Contents

Creative thinking 4

Basic cardmaking 6

Comedy fruit cards 8

Dangly cut-out cards 10

Collage cards 12

Message cards 14

Monster cards 16

Pop-up cards 18

Patterned giftwrap 20

Splatter giftwrap 22

Matching tags 24

Open-out tags 26

Ribbon rosettes and 3D stars 28

Equipment tips 30

Glossary 31

Index 32

Words in **bold** are in the glossary on page 31.

Creative thinking

We all give people greetings cards and wrap up gifts throughout the year. All those cards and sheets of wrapping paper can be expensive! And, sometimes, you just can't find cards or giftwrap that you really like. Why not try making them instead?

Get the gear!

For making cards and wrapping paper, you need basic art and craft materials such as card, paper, pens and pencils, paint, glue and scissors. Some projects use a bit of fabric or felt, and a few beads or buttons. You may have most of these things at home. If not, craft shops, toy shops, department stores and stationer's sell them quite cheaply. For help with finding particular items, see the equipment tips on page 30.

Why do it?

Besides saving money, creating your own cards and giftwrap makes them unique and special. Plus it's fun to do! If you really enjoy it, maybe you could even become a designer one day.

Safety

Remember to keep sharp scissors, craft knives, string and buttons away from small children.

Happy
Birthday
Mum!

Get well soon

Tip!
You can often reuse and recycle old bits and bobs when you're making cards. Keep old magazines, giftwrap, packaging card and paper, fabric scraps, buttons and bits of ribbon to use when you need them.

Tip!
Store all your craft gear in a shoebox or plastic container, along with finished cards and wrapping paper that are ready to use.

5

Basic cardmaking

Making a basic card isn't difficult, but it will look best if you follow these tips. Decorate it using one of the ideas below, or use it for one of the other card projects in this book.

- Thin white or coloured card, ideally in small, easy-to-use sheets (A5 size is ideal)
- Standard-sized envelope
- Ruler
- Pencil
- Scissors
- Glue
- Paper, pens, paints, photos or other materials for decorating

1 If possible, use card and envelopes that fit together, so that when the card is folded in half, it will fit in the envelope.

Tip!
If the card isn't a good fit, first measure your envelope, and mark a rectangle on the card that is about 1cm shorter and narrower than the envelope. Add another rectangle the same next to it, and cut the whole shape out.

2 Lay your piece of card flat and find the middle by measuring it. Place the ruler along the middle line, and **score** it by running the blunt outer edge of your scissors along it, pressing on the card gently.

3

You should now be able to fold your card neatly along the scored line.

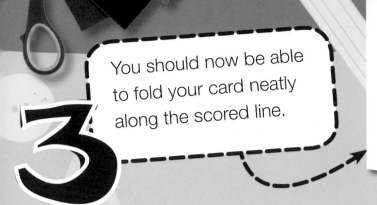

Your design will go here, on the front of the card.

4

Check your card fits into your envelope, and you're ready to go!

Tip!
You can also buy ready-made blank cards and envelopes at craft shops.

Ideas for decorating a basic card

Draw or paint a picture, cut it out, and stick it to the front of your card.

Glue on a paper or fabric shape, or small buttons or **sequins**.

Use a rubber stamp and ink to decorate your card.

Cut out a photo and glue it to the front of your card.

Happy Valentine's day!

Happy Birthday!

Comedy fruit cards

These are easy to make and suitable for any occasion. Make them as silly as you like!

- Plain basic card and envelope
- Computer and printer, or food photos from magazines or food packaging
- Scissors
- Glue
- Felt-tip pens
- Stick-on **googly eyes**

1 Find a clear, simple photo of a fruit or vegetable in a magazine or on food packaging. If you have a computer and printer, you could look for a photo on the Internet and print it out in colour. It needs to be a little smaller than your card.

2 Carefully cut out your fruit or vegetable with scissors.

3 Glue it to the front of your card, and let it dry.

Now give the fruit or vegetable a funny personality by adding stick-on googly eyes (or just draw eyes on). You can also use a felt-tip pen to add a smile, arms and legs, a hat, glasses, alien tentacles or whatever you like!

Tip!

Here are some tips for drawing cartoon faces:

- Make eyes look in different directions.

- Slanted eyebrows look cross or sad.

- High-up, curved eyebrows look happy or surprised.

- For an open mouth, colour the inside part black.

Tip!

You could add a speech bubble too. Your fruit could be saying something funny, or a message such as 'Happy Birthday'.

happy birthday

Dangly cut-out cards

These clever cards flutter and spin as you walk past. Use a shape to match the occasion, such as a heart for Valentine's Day, a star for Christmas, or a little house for moving home.

Get the gear!

- Plain basic card and envelope
- Compass or round object to draw around
- Plain white, coloured or patterned card
- Scissors or a craft knife
- Pencil
- Glue
- Fine sewing thread
- Sticky tape

1 Take your blank card and draw a large circle on the front in pencil (use a compass or draw around a round object). Carefully cut out the circle with scissors or a craft knife (ask an adult for help) to leave a hole.

2 Take a separate piece of card and fold it in half. Draw a simple shape, such as a heart, that is a little smaller than the circle you have already cut out.

3 Cut out the shape through both layers of card, so that you have two matching shapes.

4 Cut a piece of sewing thread about 6cm long. Glue it to one of your shapes, then glue the other shape on top, sandwiching the thread inside.

5 Open your card and lay it flat. Lay your shape in the middle of the circle-shaped hole, with the thread at the top. Tape the thread to the card above the hole, so that the shape hangs in the hole.

Shape ideas
Here are some more ideas for the cut-out shapes. You can decorate the shape with felt tips, paint, glitter or sequins too (do both sides).

Star	Easter egg
House	Cupcake
Bird	Smiley

Tip!
Carefully lay the shape flat when you're putting the card into its envelope.

Collage cards

Collage is a form of art where shapes, pictures, fabrics and other bits and bobs are stuck together to make a design or picture.

Get the gear!

- Plain basic card and envelope
- Scissors
- Glue
- Photos, magazines, postcards and old cards and giftwrap you can cut up
- Buttons, beads, sequins, glitter, stickers, feathers, fabric scraps, string etc.

1 Think about who, or what, the card is for, and what **theme** you want (see box on page 13). Look for pictures in magazines, stickers, fabrics or other bits and bobs to suit your theme. Cut out any pictures or shapes you need.

2 Lay your blank card flat and try arranging your pieces on the front. Move them around until you're happy with them.

3 Use glue to stick your pieces to the card or on top of each other.

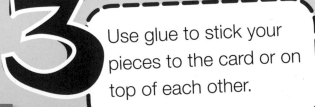

Theme and ideas

Here are some suggestions for collage cards:

Moving house

Cut up an old map or print one out from the Internet, showing the area where the new house is. Stick on cut-out house pictures, flowers and people or pets. Make a Sun from a button, or a rainbow from paper or string.

Party princess

Cut out a glamorous dress from a magazine and decorate it with sequins, ribbons, glitter or beads. Stick it over a photo of your friend to make them into a party princess!

Space theme

Use sequins and buttons to make stars, planets and comets, with string for planetary rings and comets' tails. Add a spacecraft cut out from a magazine.

Happy birthday

Cut a cake shape from patterned paper, and use felt, beads, sequins and cut-up drinking straws to make icing, decorations and candles.

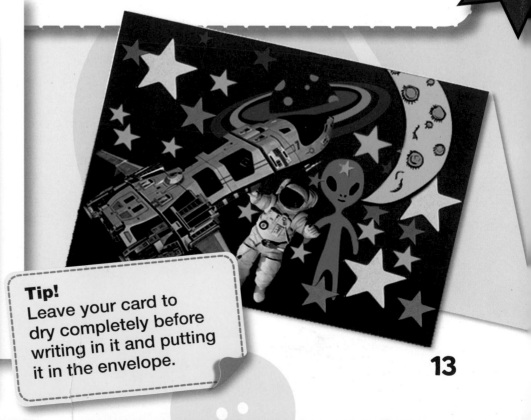

Tip!
Leave your card to dry completely before writing in it and putting it in the envelope.

13

Message cards

Cards often have a message on the front – for example, Happy Birthday, Thank You, Good Luck or Get Well Soon.

Here are some ideas for making funky message cards:

- Plain basic card and envelope
- Scissors
- Glue
- Alphabet buttons or beads, dry alphabet pasta or alphabet sweets
- OR Newspapers to cut up
- OR Computer and printer

Spell it out

You can buy little beads and buttons with letters on them, or use letter sweets or dry alphabet pasta pieces. Use strong glue to fix them to the front of your card to spell out a message.

In the news

Cut or tear headlines out of a newspaper or use individual letters to spell out a message or funny 'ransom note'.

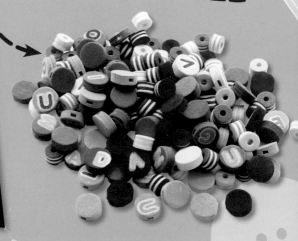

Computer design

Another great way to create stylish text is using a computer and printer. Use a program such as Word to write your message; then try changing the **font**, size and colour of the letters. When it's ready, print out your message, trim it to fit and glue it onto your card.

Some fonts have outline letter shapes that you could colour in.

come to our party!

Congratulations!

Tip!
You can combine a message with a picture, or any of the other card styles in this book.

70 Today gran

Monster cards

Make a hairy, scary card that will watch you from the mantelpiece!

Get the gear!

- Plain basic card and envelope
- Scissors
- Glue
- Small piece of fake fur fabric about the same size as your card
- 2 or more stick-on googly eyes
- Extra decorations such as pipe cleaners, stickers, buttons, sequins or string

1 Cut out a monster from your furry fabric. It could be round, sausage-shaped, blob-shaped or any shape you like!

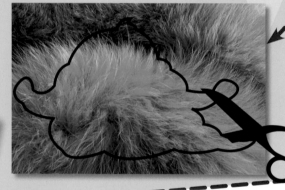

2 Cover the back of the fabric in glue and stick it firmly to the front of your card.

3 Stick on the googly eyes somewhere among the fur. More than two eyes will make it extra-monstrous!

Tip!
If you have trouble getting the googly eyes to stay on, add glue as well.

4

If you like, you can add more decorations such as pipe-cleaner tentacles or spots made from stickers, buttons or sequins.

Tip!
Another method is to trim the fake fur to the exact shape and size of the front of your card, and cover the card completely. Stick the googly eyes near the top.

Tip!
If you can't find fake fur, you could use velvet, fleece or felt fabric.

Pop-up cards

When you open these cards, a 3D shape pops up!

You will need:

- Plain basic card and envelope
- Scissors
- Glue
- Thin, plain white card
- Felt-tip pens or other decorations such as glitter

1 Measure the width of your blank card. Cut a strip of plain card that is as long as this, and about 2cm wide.

2cm

2 Fold over a flap at each end of the strip, about 1cm in. Then make another fold 2cm from one end, like this.

3 Open your card out and lay it flat. Take your strip and fold the two 1cm flaps under. Position the strip on the card so that the left edge (which is tucked underneath) lines up with the middle of the card. The strip should lie flat. Glue the flaps to the card, pressing down hard, then leave to dry.

4 When your card is dry, check you can open and close it. The strip should lift up when you open the card.

5 Now draw a shape or picture on another piece of card, colour and decorate it, and cut it out. It should be narrower than the width of your card.

6 Glue your shape to the flat part of the card strip. When it's dry, open your card to see your design pop up!

Tip!
For tricky ideas, make a test version in plain card first to check it works.

More ideas

Here are some ideas for pop-up card pictures:

- A star, moon, snowflake or candle
- A spider, ghost, pumpkin or witch for Halloween
- A rocket, plane or hot-air balloon
- A heart for Valentine's Day
- A coloured-in, cut-out word or phrase, such as Party! or Boo!

Patterned giftwrap

Homemade giftwrap is easy and cheap to make – and you'll never run out! Making your own wrapping paper also means you can tailor it for any occasion or for a particular person.

You'll need:

- Plain white or coloured paper
- Felt-tip pens or other decorations
- OR Rubber stamps
- OR Paint

Tip!
It's easiest to use large pieces of paper to start with. IKEA® and some craft shops sell big rolls of plain art paper, or you could use **lining paper** from a DIY shop. If you only have smaller sheets of paper, stick a few together with sticky tape.

Get doodling

Use felt tips to decorate your plain paper with a pattern all over, such as coloured wavy lines, dots, squares, eyes, little spirals or doodles.

Happy Birthday!
Happy Birthday!
Happy Birthday!
Happy Birthday!
Happy Birthday!
Happy Birthday!
Happy Birthday!
Happy Birthday!
Happy Birthday!
Happy Birthday!
Happy Birthday!
Happy Birthday!

Message paper

Write a message such as Happy Birthday, Good Luck, New Home or New Baby all over the paper in different colours, sizes and styles of writing.

Print pattern

Use a rubber stamp and ink to cover the paper in a repeated shape.

Splatter giftwrap

This is a fun and easy way to make colourful giftwrap that looks splatastic!

You will need:

- Plain white or coloured paper
- Old newspaper and old clothes
- Old toothbrush
- Watery poster paint in several colours

1 Spread out the old newspaper on the floor, and lay your plain paper on top. Make sure you're well away from furniture and wearing old clothes.

2

Dip the toothbrush in paint and press it with your thumb, like this, to spray splats of paint across the paper.

3

Cover the paper with lots of splats of different colours. Rinse the toothbrush clean with water before changing to a new colour.

4

Once you're happy with how it looks, leave the paper to dry completely.

Tip!
You can make cool splatter shapes by using **stencils**. Cut a shape out of card to make a stencil. Lay your stencil on the paper and splatter paint over it. Carefully remove the stencil.

Tip!
Cut your splatter paper into smaller pieces and use them to make cards.

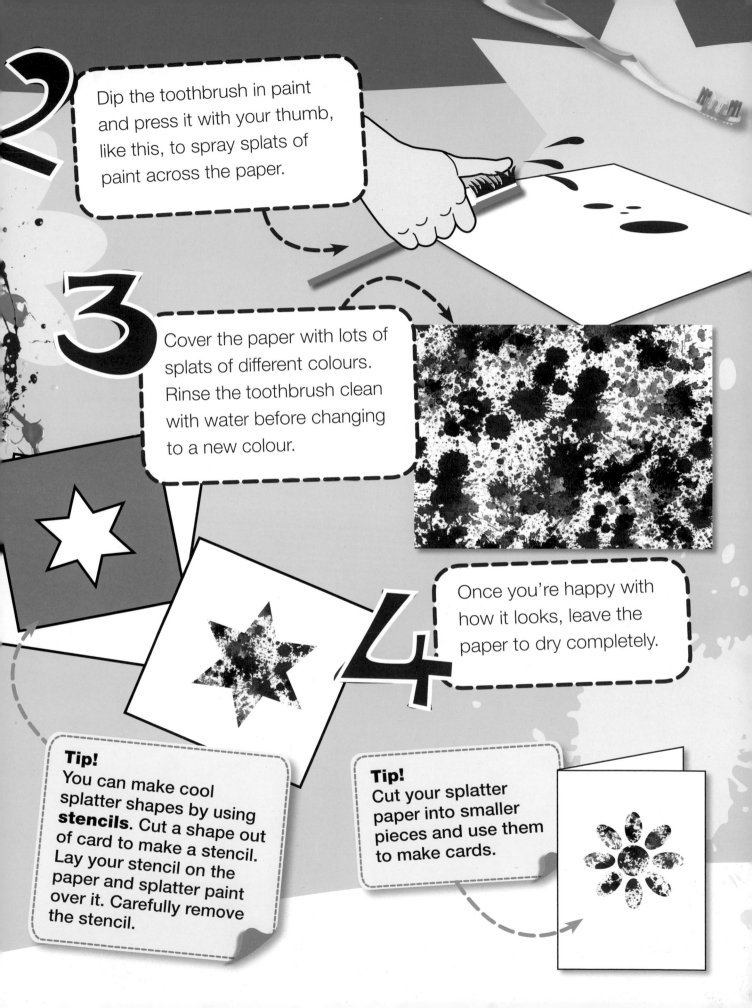

Matching tags

To make your wrapped presents look extra-fancy and professional, make gift tags that match your wrapping paper.

- Plain white or coloured card
- Pencil
- Scissors
- Hole punch
- Narrow ribbon or coloured thread

1 To make your tags, draw simple rectangles or other shapes on the card. Make each tag about 6–8cm long.

2 Cut out your tag shapes with scissors. Use the hole punch to make a hole in one end or corner of each tag.

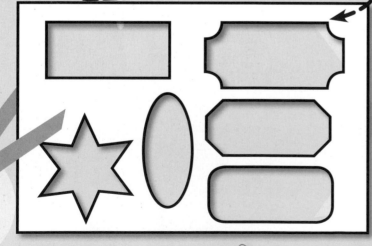

3

Decorate the tag to match the giftwrap you are making. If you're making patterned paper (see pages 20–21), draw or print the same pattern onto your tags. If you're making splatter paper (see pages 22–23), lay the tags down next to your paper so they get splatted too.

4

When the tags are finished and dry, add the ribbon or thread. Cut a piece of ribbon or thread about 12cm long and thread it through the hole in the tag. Then tie or sticky tape it to a wrapped present, and write your message on the blank side.

Tag shapes

Here are some tag shapes to copy:

Heart
Easter egg
Star
Flower
Leaf
Snowman

Tip!
Make two or three tags for each sheet of giftwrap you make, and you should always have enough for all your presents.

Open-out tags

These cool gift labels open out to reveal your surprise message.

You will need:

- Plain white, coloured or shiny card
- Pencil
- Scissors
- Glue
- Felt-tip pens

1 Copy one of these shapes onto your card. You can make them this size, or up to 15cm across.

2 Cut out the shape carefully with scissors, and fold in the star points or petals along the dotted lines.

3 Colour in the inside and outside of the points or petals with plain colours or patterns.

Write your message in the middle, then fold in the points or petals. They will cover the message, but stick up to make a 3D shape. They can be opened out to read the message.

happy birthday mum!

4

Tip!
Use colours that contrast with your giftwrap, so the tag stands out.

5

Glue the back of the tag to your present, leaving the flaps free.

Tip!
Try designing your own versions based on the same basic template. What about a Sun, a starfish or a spider? Or try making bigger or smaller versions, or using patterned card.

Ribbon rosettes and 3D stars

It's easy to make funky **rosette** or star decorations to stick onto your presents. They look brilliant and they're much cheaper than the ones in the shops!

Get the gear!

- Coloured, shiny or metallic paper or thin card
- Pencil
- Ruler
- Scissors
- Spare buttons, beads, stickers, or stick-on flowers

Paper ribbon rosette

1 Cut four strips of paper or card, each about 2cm wide and 20cm long.

2 Take one strip, pull the ends up and in and glue them to the middle, like this. (If the paper is coloured or shiny on only one side, make that the outside.)

3 Repeat with all the strips; then stick them on top of each other, like this.

4 Stick a pretty button, bead, sticker or just a circle of paper in the middle. Now glue onto a present!

Tip!
If your glue doesn't hold the rosette together properly, you can staple it through the middle before sticking on the decoration.

3D star

1 Copy this template onto coloured or shiny paper or thin card, and cut it out.

2 Fold your star in half along the three dotted lines shown here, unfolding it again each time.

3 Then turn your star over and fold along these three dotted lines.

4 You should now be able to squeeze your star into a 3D shape. Then glue or sticky-tape it to a present.

Equipment tips

Here are some tips on the types of materials and equipment you might need, and where to find them.

Beads
Craft shops, toy shops and sewing shops often have beads, and there are also specialist bead shops. You can reuse beads from old or broken jewellery too.

Buttons
You can buy buttons in sewing shops, craft shops and department stores. Also try charity shops and reusing buttons from old clothes.

Card
Art, craft, stationery and toy shops are all good places to find white and coloured card for making your basic cards.

Envelopes
From stationer's, supermarkets and post offices.

Fake fur fabric
Fabric shops, craft shops and some department stores sell fake fur.

Felt
Fabric shops, department stores, craft shops and toy shops often have felt.

Googly eyes
Craft shops, toy shops and stationery shops sell these in little bags.

Lining paper or paper on rolls
DIY shops sell rolls of plain white lining paper, perfect for making wrapping paper. IKEA® is also good for large rolls of plain paper.

Online
There are many fabric and craft shops on the Internet. You may find the following sites useful starting points:
www.handyhippo.co.uk
www.hobbycraft.co.uk
www.myfabrics.co.uk

Paints and paintbrushes
Art shops and toy shops are good for paint – it's usually cheaper in toy shops.

Paper
For plain white and coloured paper, look in toy shops and stationery shops. Specialist craft shops and art shops often have more interesting options, such as textured and patterned paper.

Pencils, felt-tips, glue, ruler
Most stationery shops and toy shops have these, if you don't have them around at home. It's best to use PVA or strong paper glue.

Ready-made blank cards and matching envelopes
Craft shops and some stationery shops have these.

Ribbons
Sewing and fabric shops usually sell ribbons and trimmings by the metre.

Scissors
The sharper your scissors, the easier they are to work with, but take care when using them.

Sequins
You can often find these at craft shops and stationer's.

Sewing thread
Sewing shops and department stores usually have sewing thread in lots of colours.

Stick-on flowers, letters and shapes
From craft shops and stationer's.

Glossary

collage
A form of art in which photos, fabric and other items are stuck down to make a picture or design.

font
A style of lettering.

googly eyes
Small stick-on plastic eyes with moving pupils, for craft projects.

lining paper
Plain white wallpaper.

rosette
Decorative flower made of ribbon, fabric or paper.

score
To cut or scratch into a surface.

sequins
Little shiny or metallic discs with a hole in the middle.

stencil
A cut-out shape for colouring or painting through.

theme
A subject or topic.

Index

3D shapes
18, 27, 29
3D stars
29

beads
4, 12, 13, 14, 28
birthdays
9, 13, 14, 21
buttons
4, 5, 7, 12, 13, 14, 16, 17, 28

cards
4, 5, 6–19, 23
　basic
　6–7
　collage
　12–13
　comedy fruit
　8–9
　dangly cut-out
　10–11
　message
　14–15
　monster
　16–17
　pop-up
　18–19
Christmas
10
craft knives
4, 10
craft shops
4

department stores
4
DIY shops
20

fabric
4, 5, 7, 12, 17
fake fur
16
feathers
12
felt
4, 13, 17
felt tips
11, 18
fleece
17
fonts
15

giftwrap
4, 5, 20–23, 24, 25, 27
　message
　21
　patterned
　20–21, 25
　splatter
　22–23, 25
glitter
11, 13
googly eyes
8, 9, 16

Halloween
19

ink
7, 21

lining paper
20

magazines
5, 8, 12, 13
moving house
10, 13, 21

new baby
21
new home
see moving house
newspapers
14, 22

paint
11, 20, 22, 23
photos
6, 8, 12, 13
pipe cleaners
16, 17

recycling
5
ribbon rosettes
28
ribbons
5, 13, 25

sequins
7, 11, 12, 13, 16, 17
stamps, rubber
7, 20, 21, 25

stationery shops
4
stencils
23
stickers
12, 16, 17, 28
string
4, 12, 13, 16

tags
　matching
　24–25
　open-out
　26–27
toy shops
4

Valentine's Day
10, 19
velvet
17

wrapping paper
see giftwrap